I0167529

Freddie and His Ocean Friends

This course was written by
Naturally Curious Expert
Tucker Hirsch

*Tucker is a marine scientist who is curious about
the lives and future of our ocean friends.*

Printed by CreateSpace

ISBN 978-1-942403-06-7

www.benaturallycurious.com

Many activities in this book make use of printed materials. If you prefer not to cut them directly from this book, please visit the URL listed below and enter the code for a supplemental PDF containing all printable materials.

URL: www.benaturallycurious.com/ocean-friends-printables/

password: **plankton**

Table of Contents

Required materials: water, scissors, tape, blank paper, paper clips, string or yarn, coloring materials (crayons, paint, markers), empty shoe box, hole punch (optional), 8 stuffed animals (or friends), various small household items (floaty bath toys, paper clips, corks, erasers, clay, toothpicks, etc.), small bowl or container, larger bucket (~5 gallon) or tank

Freddie and His Ocean Friends

Freddie is a fish. He lives in the ocean. This morning, Freddie swam to his dad with some very peculiar questions.

"Dad," began Freddie, "why don't I look like you? Will I ever look like you? Why are we different?"

Freddie's dad gave a bubbly-fish sigh and told Freddie, "Son, let's take a look at the family photo album."

Freddie and his dad started looking at pictures of family and friends, and Freddie began to learn a lot about himself and also about the ocean around him. Let's go listen in…

"Hey, look!" cried Freddie. "There I am at Christmas! And there are my friends! I never realized how different we all look. So many different shapes and sizes."

"That's right," Freddie's dad replied. "You are all different. Even your cousins—who are all flatfish— look different. You're all different ages, and you're all at different stages of your LIFE CYCLE."

His dad explained further: Freddie, his cousins, his mom, and his dad are all flounders—a type of fish that lives in the ocean. Freddie looks like lots of other fish in the ocean—one fin on each side, one eye on each side, and both of his sides look the same.

Freddie. Christmas 2012

But Freddie's mom and dad lie down to swim, with both eyes on the same side, and one fin—the top one—much bigger than the other fin.

"Life cycle?" asked Freddie. "Does that mean we won't live very long?"

"Don't worry! A life cycle is all the different stages or shapes you'll go through between being an egg and an adult," Freddie's dad started to explain. "Lots of fish look very different as JUVENILES and as adults. You started as a very small fish egg. You couldn't swim at all—you just floated around in the currents. You were called PLANKTON because you couldn't swim. All the living things in the ocean that can't swim are called plankton. They just get pushed around in the water and go with the flow."

Freddie's dad explained that as Freddie grew to be a bigger plankton, he started looking more like a tadpole, and eventually like a little fish. He was starting to swim better and better.

Mom and Dad. Dancing at the New Year's Eve Ball, 2012

An animal's *life cycle* is all the different changes it goes through from juvenile to adult.

All the living things in the ocean that can't swim are called *plankton*.

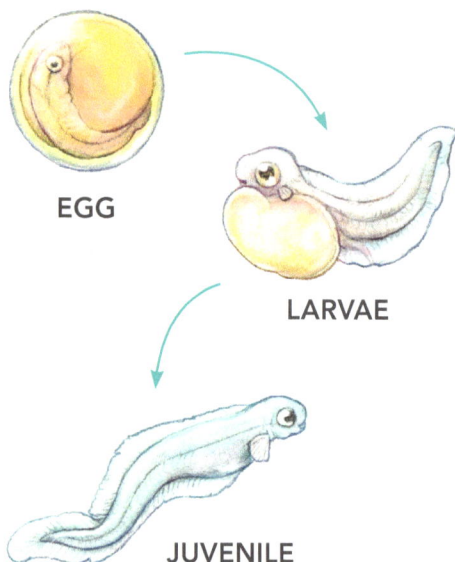

EGG

LARVAE

JUVENILE

What are you CURIOUS about?

Eventually, Freddie's dad explained, Freddie would go through a bigger change—a **METAMORPHOSIS**—where he would lose all his young fish parts and turn into an adult. Because Freddie was a flounder, this meant that one eye would actually move, over many days, onto the other side of his body! His fin on that side would become very strong, and the fin where his eye used to be would get smaller and weaker because he wouldn't need it anymore. At that time, Freddie would start swimming on his side, just like his mom and dad. And he would be a very good swimmer.

"So will I still be a plankton?" asked Freddie.

"No, Freddie. The animals in the ocean that are *strong* swimmers are called **NEKTON**."

Freddie also noticed other differences. He ate different foods than his dad ate.

"Right now, Freddie, you eat very little things. You actually eat *other* plankton. When you become a nekton, you will be a strong swimmer, and you can swim after your food. Then you can eat other small fish and larger food."

Freddie thought that this was a lot of information to take in, so his dad drew a little diagram to show him some of the steps of a flounder's metamorphosis:

Some animals change how their bodies look through a process called *metamorphosis*.

All the animals in the ocean that are strong swimmers are called *nekton*.

What are you CURIOUS about?

"What about my food, Dad?" Freddie asked, worried that he wouldn't be able to eat his favorite plankton any more.

"The littlest things get eaten by something bigger, and the bigger things get eaten by the biggest thing," his dad explained. "That's why you eat little plankton, I eat small nekton, and we both need to look out for the large PREDATORS. Predators are any animals that eat other animals. Right now, you are a predator of the plankton. When you get bigger, you will be a predator of other, bigger food."

"So... sharks are predators?" asked Freddie.

"Yes, Freddie. Sharks are predators. And since predators such as sharks would like to eat us, we are also PREY. We have to look out for the bigger fish that like to eat us. We're all linked together, like a chain."

"A FOOD CHAIN!" exclaimed Freddie. "When one animal eats another animal that eats ANOTHER animal..."

"Exactly! That's called a food chain," Freddie's dad assured him.

Freddie shuddered, thinking of the sharks that lived in his part of the ocean. He knew he had colors that helped camouflage himself in the sand, but he also knew he had to be careful and always look out for bigger fish.

Even though two animals may be the same type (for example, flounder), one might be a plankton and one might be a nekton, depending on how strong a swimmer each one is.

Predators are any animals that eat other animals for food.

Prey are any animals that get eaten by other animals.

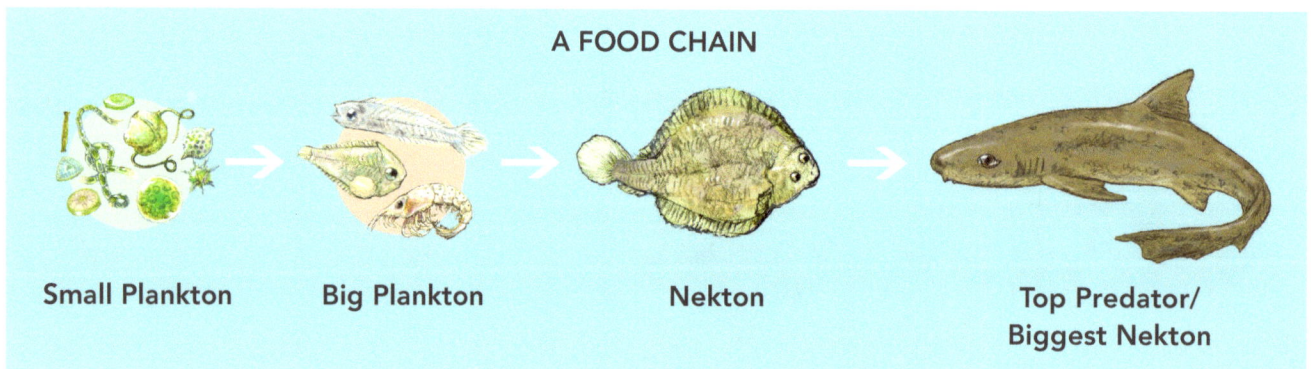

A FOOD CHAIN

Small Plankton → Big Plankton → Nekton → Top Predator/ Biggest Nekton

"Is everyone a predator?" Freddie wondered. He knew everyone had to eat.

"Some things in the ocean can make their own food," Freddie's dad told him, "the way the plants on land use sunlight to make food. These are a type of plankton called PHYTOPLANKTON and we call them PRODUCERS. They can't swim, and they don't eat other things in the ocean. They use the sun's energy to get all the energy they need."

Freddie's dad reviewed the plankton for Freddie: There are two different types of plankton: phytoplankton and ZOOPLANKTON. The phytoplankton are producers that make their own food from the sun. The zooplankton eat other plankton, so they are predators, or CONSUMERS.

Many animals are BOTH predators and prey.

Living things that don't eat other plants or animals are called *producers*.

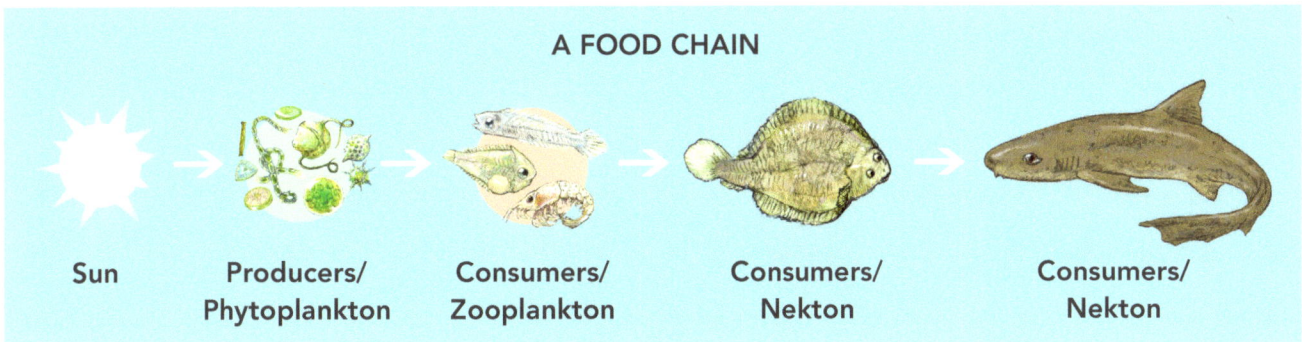

A FOOD CHAIN

| Sun | Producers/ Phytoplankton | Consumers/ Zooplankton | Consumers/ Nekton | Consumers/ Nekton |

What are you CURIOUS about?

ZOOPLANKTON

PHYTOPLANKTON

There are actually LOTS of types of plankton. The word *plankton* is sort of like the word *dog*—there are Labradors and golden retrievers and huskies and Chihuahuas, but they're all dogs. There are many types of zooplankton and phytoplankton with many different names, but they're all plankton because they can't swim.

"But Dad, Mom says we don't have to worry about some of the biggest animals in the ocean because they won't eat us," Freddie interrupted.

"Ah, your mom is right! Some of the biggest animals in the ocean—the whales—eat the smallest nekton and the plankton. But other whales *do* eat bigger fish. There are many different food chains in the ocean."

"Yeah! And some animals *outside* of the ocean eat the big nekton, like when birds eat fish!" exclaimed Freddie.

What are you CURIOUS about?

"**Y**ou're right, Freddie. Let's look at our food chain and the food chains that some of your friends are part of," suggested Freddie's dad.

"But Dad, this is kind of sad. We're talking about eating other animals and even other animals eating us!" Freddie cried.

"It's true, Freddie. Everything in the ocean must eat. We are all food for other animals, and others are food for us," Freddie's dad explained.

"I guess it's fair. The ocean is in a balance. If no one ate the flounders, there wouldn't be enough food for all of us."

"And that's why food chains are so important," said Freddie's dad. "Now, how about a snack before bedtime?"

"Sure! I want some zooplankton!"

What are you CURIOUS about?

Which of these would you call predators? Prey? Plankton?

Flinking!

Now that you know about Freddie, you know that he is in his plankton stage. Freddie will go through a metamorphosis and grow into a nekton. Some of his friends will also grow out of their plankton stage, but others will not. (And, remember too, that Freddie is the type of plankton called *zooplankton* because he cannot make his own food.)

Let's see how Freddie lives. He and his plankton buddies like to float. The currents they need in order to move through the ocean are best near the surface. If they sink too deep in the ocean, they can't get enough sunlight. Also, the phytoplankton that they like to eat stay near the top to get enough sunlight, too. But, if they bob right up to the surface, they can get too much sun. Can you build a plankton that doesn't float *and* doesn't sink? Maybe it should be called *flinking* or *soating*!

INSTRUCTIONS

Collect some things from around your house that are okay to get wet (you can ask an adult to help you). Fill a small bowl with water and test to see if your items sink or float.

Once you have a good mix of items, start to create your own plankton. Your goal is to make something that starts to sink but never touches the bottom. You can tie more than one object together with string to make a new object.

When your plankton creation is complete, fill the large bucket with water and see how your plankton performs! If your plankton floats on the top or sinks to the bottom, make some changes to help it stay in the middle. Keep testing and changing your plankton until it's just right.

MATERIALS

- small bowl or container
- larger bucket (~5 gallons), aquarium tank, plastic file bin, or other similar container
- various household items (e.g. floaty bath toys, paper clips, corks, erasers, clay, washers, beads, toothpicks)
- string or yarn
- water (enough to fill the containers)

Flinking!

INSTRUCTIONS (continued)

Challenge: Make it a plankton race! Find a friend who can also make a *flinking* plankton. On the count of three, place both of your plankton creations in the water at the same time. See which plankton stays in the middle of bucket of water. The first one to float up to the surface or touch the bottom is out!

Don't have a friend around? Make two plankton yourself or time just one creation. See how long your plankton can *flink*!

As you try out different objects, make sure to record your findings in the Experimental Journal on page 14. You can give each type of plankton a name, describe what objects you used to make it, why you picked those objects, and what those objects did when you dropped them in the water (Did they float? Did they sink to the bottom?). For each plankton you test, what is your conclusion? A conclusion is what you learn from each experiment you do!

After you fill out your Experimental Journal, pick your favorite plankton! Draw a picture of it on page 15 and answer the questions.

Remember to clean up when you're done. Make sure to wipe up any water, dry the buckets, and put away the household items.

Parents' Tips

- Small corks are a great material for kids to start with. Most household items sink, but a cork is very buoyant. One cork with many other items often works well.

- Sometimes a small change is all that's needed. A cork with three washers may sink straight to the bottom. But if you take off one washer, the creation may pop right back to the top. Help children make small changes.

ACTIVITY 1

Experimental Journal

Plankton 1

Name: _____

What is it made of? _____

Why did you choose it? _____

How did it behave? _____

Conclusion: _____

Plankton 2

Name: _____

What is it made of? _____

Why did you choose it? _____

How did it behave? _____

Conclusion: _____

Plankton 3

Name: _____

What is it made of? _____

Why did you choose it? _____

How did it behave? _____

Conclusion: _____

Plankton 4

Name: _____

What is it made of? _____

Why did you choose it? _____

How did it behave? _____

Conclusion: _____

ACTIVITY 1

Experimental Journal

Draw a picture of the plankton you created.

What is your plankton called? _____

What do you imagine your plankton would eat? _____

What do you imagine your plankton's predator would be? _____

Tangled Up in Food Webs

ACTIVITY 2

Now you're familiar with food chains—predators eat prey. But think back to Freddie. He told his dad he wanted zooplankton for a snack after looking at the family album. Freddie likes other things to eat, too. And, just as Freddie likes lots of different foods, many different predators would eat Freddie if they had the chance. Predators and prey don't always form a single food chain. They usually form a food web.

Let's start with a medium-sized fish. This fish would eat small fish. But it might also eat zooplankton. Big fish would probably eat the medium fish. But so could birds, people, seals, sea lions, and maybe polar bears, depending on where the medium fish lived.

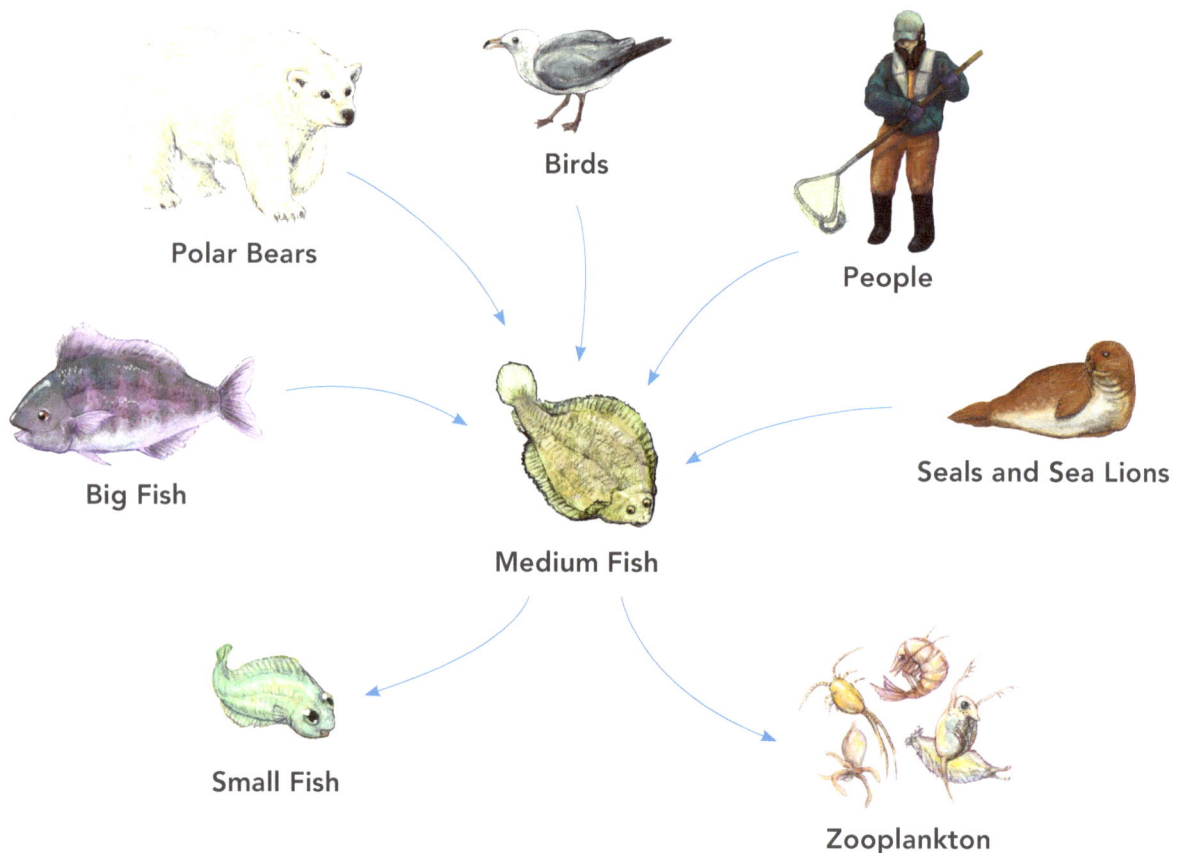

Polar Bears

Birds

People

Big Fish

Seals and Sea Lions

Medium Fish

Small Fish

Zooplankton

This is a very simple food web. Many more kinds of animals live in the sea! And many more kinds of animals could be connected! If you tried to add all the animals into the same food web, it would be very large and complicated.

Now it's your turn to create a food web.

Tangled Up in Food Webs

ACTIVITY
2

INSTRUCTIONS

Find eight friends and family members, or use toys or stuffed animals.

1. Print out the cards on page 31.

2. Using a hole punch, create a hole in the top of each card where the circle is. If you don't have a hole punch, you can push a paper clip through the card. Tie a piece of string through the hole or paper clip to make the card into a necklace. Give one to each person (or stuffed animal). Have the friends or stuffed animals make a circle.

3. Ask each person to read their card and memorize who their animal would eat. Then, each person should find their **prey** and hold hands (or feet) with it. If you are using stuffed animals, use a piece of string to tie the **predator** to its **prey.**

4. Be careful! You will probably end up with a spider web.

Before you let go of your friends or stuffed animals, draw the food web you created.

MATERIALS

- hole punch (or 8 paper clips)
- scissors
- string
- 8 friends or stuffed animals

ACTIVITY
3

A Food Chain Card Game

INSTRUCTIONS

In this activity, you will mix and match different ocean animals to build different food chains.

MATERIALS

- scissors
- 1 set of Fish Food Chain Cards
- 1 set of Fish Bonus Cards (optional)

Instructions for Younger Players:

1. Cut out the cards on pages 33 and 35.

2. Set the Bonus Cards aside. Shuffle or mix all the Fish Food Chain Cards. Place the pile of Fish Food Chain Cards face down on a flat playing surface.

3. Players take turns drawing cards from the deck and playing them face up on the table.

4. Use the Food Chain Guide to see if your card connects to another card that is face up on the table. If you draw a card that is exactly one above or one below another card face up on the table, according to the Food Chain Guide, place your card next to the card that has already been played.

5. If you draw a card that completes a food chain, according to the Food Chain Guide, take the entire food chain and place it on the table in front of you. You have won a food chain!

6. If all the parts of a food chain are on the table, but not connected, and you draw a card that will complete the food chain, you may move the other cards needed to complete the food chain. You have won a food chain! You can ONLY move cards that have already been played if you are going to compete a food chain.

7. When all the cards have been played, count your score, according to the Food Chain Guide.

8. The player with the highest score is the Food Chain Champion!

Instructions for Older Players:

1. Cut out the cards on pages 33 and 35.

2. Shuffle or mix all the Fish Food Chain Cards. Set the Fish Bonus Cards aside. Lay the Fish Food Chain Cards spread out and face down on a flat playing surface.

3. Players take turns drawing cards from the face down cards and placing them face up in front of themselves on the table. Players can only add to their own food chains, not to the food chains of other players.

4. If you draw a card that is exactly one above or one below another card in front of you, according to the Food Chain Guide, place the two cards next to each other.

ACTIVITY
3

A Food Chain Card Game

INSTRUCTIONS (continued)

5. If you draw a card that completes one of your food chains, according to the Food Chain Guide, collect all the cards in that food chain and set them aside.

6. Players can change combinations in their face up cards at any time and as often as they want. They cannot change completed food chains.

7. When all the cards have been played, count your score, according to the Food Chain Guide.

Food Chain Guide

Possible Food Chain Creations   **Points**

Phytoplankton – Zooplankton – Whale   2 Points

Phytoplankton – Zooplankton – Small Fish – Medium Fish – Big Fish – Shark   1 Point

Phytoplankton – Zooplankton – Baby Fish – Medium Fish – Big Fish – Shark   1 Point

Jelly – Turtle – Shark   2 Points

* Add an extra point if you have Freddie in your food chain!

A Food Chain Card Game

ACTIVITY
3

INSTRUCTIONS (continued)

Bonus Round for Older Players

1. Shuffle and mix all the Food Chain Cards and the Bonus Food Chain Cards together. Follow instructions for younger players.

2. Use the guides for the Bonus Food Chains.

Bonus: Possible Food Chain Creations	Points
Phytoplankton – Zooplankton – Whale – People	1 Point
Phytoplankton – Zooplankton – Small Fish – People	1 Point
Phytoplankton – Zooplankton – Small Fish – Birds	1 Point
Phytoplankton – Zooplankton – Small Fish – Medium Fish – People	1 Point
Phytoplankton – Zooplankton – Small Fish – Medium Fish – Big Fish – People	1 Point
Phytoplankton – Zooplankton – Small Fish – Medium Fish – Big Fish – Shark – People	1 Point
Phytoplankton – Zooplankton – Baby Fish – People	1 Point
Phytoplankton – Zooplankton – Baby Fish – Medium Fish – People	1 Point
Phytoplankton – Zooplankton – Baby Fish – Medium Fish –Polar Bear	1 Point
Phytoplankton – Zooplankton – Baby Fish – Medium Fish – Big Fish – People	1 Point
Phytoplankton – Zooplankton – Baby Fish – Medium Fish – Big Fish – Shark – People	1 Point
Jelly – Turtle – People	1 Point
Jelly – Turtle – Shark – People	1 Point

* Add an extra point if you have Freddie in your food chain!

Parents' Tips

- Help students use the guides above. It may be helpful for each person to have a printed copy of the Possible Food Chain Creations for reference while they are playing the game.

- Before starting, look at and review the cards, and create a few sample Food Chains, based on the Possible Food Chain Creations.

- The cards are in a specific ratio. If you need more cards, print, cut out, and play with a complete second set.

ACTIVITY
3

Experimental Journal

What was the easiest food chain to complete? _____

_____

What was the hardest food chain to complete? _____

_____

Was there a card you always wanted more of? Were there too many of any card?

_____

_____

Create Your Own Metamorphosis

Remember that Freddie is a plankton right now because he can't swim. As he gets older, he will look more and more like his father. His father is a nekton because he is a strong swimmer. Freddie will go through metamorphosis as he changes. Because he is a flounder, one of his fins will get smaller and one of his eyes will move to the other side of his head!

Other animals also go through metamorphosis. Many insects—like butterflies—look very different as juveniles. They are caterpillars! Frogs also look different when they are young. They are tadpoles with tails and no legs. Both of these animals go through metamorphosis, just like Freddie.

Many other ocean animals also look very different when they are young. Here are some examples:

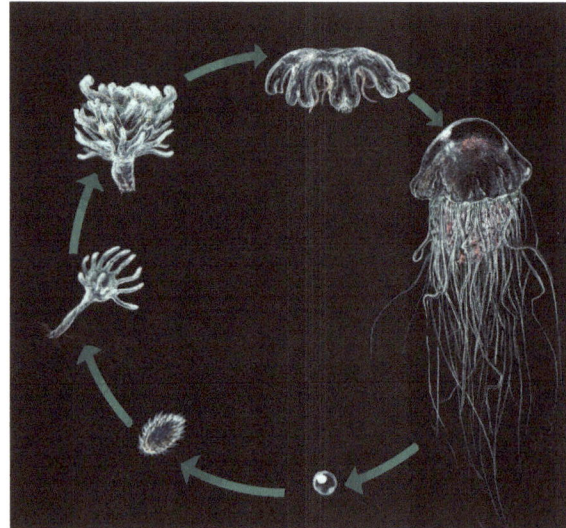

ACTIVITY 4

Create Your Own Metamorphosis

INSTRUCTIONS

Now it's your turn! Create a new, imaginary, ocean animal that starts its life looking very different from the adult. Your animal should start as juvenile, go through metamorphosis, and end up as an adult.

1. In each of the circles on page 37, draw one stage of the life cycle of your animal. The baby and the adult should share a few things—perhaps some of the same colors or the same number of legs, or a tail. But overall, they can look very different! Remember, your animal should change from a plankton to a nekton (not swimming to swimming).

2. Using the inside of the shoe box, design your animal's habitat—the place where it lives in the ocean. (You may need to cover the inside of the shoe box with white paper so you can draw on it.) You can add food that your animal will eat, any predators that might live near your animal, and anything else— like rocks, waves, seaweed, and other animals—that might live with your animal.

3. Cut out the circles.

4. Carefully make a hole near the top of each circle with a paper clip. Slide the paper clip in place.

5. Tie a piece of string to each paper clip. Tape the other end of the string to the inside top of the shoe box. Now your animal can swim or float in its habitat!

MATERIALS

- paper
- scissors
- 4 paper clips
- string
- tape
- shoe box
- coloring materials: markers, paint, or crayons

ACTIVITY
4

Experimental Journal

What is the name of the creature you created?

_____

Write about your creature. Where does it live? What does it eat?
Who are its predators?

_____

_____

_____

_____

Explain how your creature changes during metamorphosis. Which parts of it change? Which
parts stay the same? Share any other features about your creature that help it survive.

_____

_____

_____

_____

_____

Print out extra copies of page 37 and make as many new animals as you'd like!

Curiosity Connector

Here are some links to help you follow your curiosity!

- Take your food web knowledge to the next level. A very detailed and more advanced graphic on food webs:
http://education.nationalgeographic.com/education/media/coral-reef-food-web/?ar_a=1

- Like coloring? Find out who lives in different places in the ocean and color them!

  In the coral reefs:
  http://education.nationalgeographic.com/education/media/coral-reef-ecosystem/?ar_a=1

  In the kelp forest:
  http://education.nationalgeographic.com/education/media/kelp-forest-ecosystem/?ar_a=1

  And at the sandy shore:
  http://education.nationalgeographic.com/education/media/sandy-shore-ecosystem/?ar_a=1

- Compare your food web to another food web:
http://askabiologist.asu.edu/sites/default/files/resources/activities/plankton/plankton_eat_plankton_packet5.pdf

- Test your knowledge of specific food chains:
http://www.ecokids.ca/PUB/eco_info/topics/frogs/chain_reaction/play_chainreaction.cfm

- You learned about Freddie the Flatfish. Now see what some of his cousins look like while they're hiding under the sand:
http://www.nightstalkerguideservice.com/flfind.html#11

- Polar bears really are part of food chains. See them prey on, or eat, on eggs:
http://video.nationalgeographic.com/video/news/animals-news/polar-bear-predation-vin/

- Whales don't just eat krill, plankton, and small fish near the surface. They also dig in the sand on the bottom of the ocean for plankton and small fish:
http://video.nationalgeographic.com/video/news/animals-news/humpback-whales-bottom-feeding-vin/

Glossary

CONSUMERS – Animals that get energy by eating other animals. They cannot make their own food.

FOOD CHAIN – A series of living things that are each dependent on the next one as a food source.

HABITAT – The place where a plant or animal is at home and can get all its food, shelter, and water, and have its other needs met.

JUVENILES – Young animals that cannot reproduce. They may look different from their parents.

LIFE CYCLE – The changes and different phases of an animal's life, from egg to baby to juvenile to adult.

METAMORPHOSIS – A process that some animals go through to change their body shape and structures.

NEKTON – Animals in oceans, lakes, and ponds that can swim.

PHYTOPLANKTON – Nonswimming, drifting creatures that use the sun's energy and photosynthesis to get energy. They do not eat other plants or animals.

PLANKTON – Animals in oceans, lakes, and ponds that cannot swim. They drift with water currents.

PREDATORS – Animals that hunt and eat other animals for food.

PREY – An animal that is eaten by another animal.

PRODUCERS – Creatures that can make their own food from sunlight and photosynthesis.

ZOOPLANKTON – Nonswimming, drifting creatures that eat other creatures. They cannot make their own food.

Tools for Your Tool Kit

Let's make the ideas you learned today part of your life tool kit. Remember to print out some blank tool kit pages and tape or glue on today's tools.

1. Look at or listen to the following words. Circle all the ones that describe Freddie at the age he's at in the story:

   NEKTON   PRODUCER   PLANKTON   PREY   ZOOPLANKTON

   FLOUNDER   PHYTOPLANKTON   CONSUMER   SHARK   ADULT   PREDATOR

   Add a FLATFISH to your tool kit!

2. Arrange the following organisms into one food chain:

   Big Fish   Plankton   Small Fish   Shark

   _____

   Add FOOD CHAIN to your tool kit!

3. Plankton are plants and the animals in the water that can't _____ .

   Add PLANKTON to your tool kit!

4. Animals that can't make their own food and that eat other animals are

   called _____ .

   Add PREDATOR to your tool kit!

5. Frogs, lobsters, and flatfish all experience a change in their body shapes during their life

   cycle. What is the name of this change? _____

   Add METAMORPHOSIS to your tool kit!

Tools for Your Tool Kit (continued)

Predator

Freddie

Phytoplankton

Metamorphosis

Food Chain

Plankton

Shark

Eats: Sea Lion, Big Fish

Sea Lion

Eats: Medium Fish

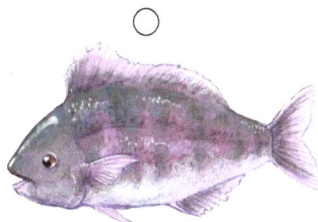

Big Fish

Eats: Medium Fish

Medium Fish

Eats: Small Fish

Bird

Eats: Medium Fish, Small Fish

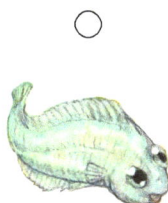

Small Fish

Eats: Plankton

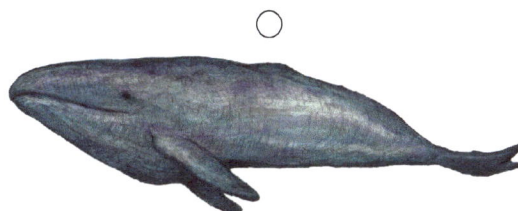

Whale

Eats: Plankton, Big Fish

Cutouts for Activity 3: A Food Chain Card Game

Phytoplankton	Zooplankton	Small Fish	Medium Fish	Shark	Jelly
Phytoplankton	Zooplankton	Small Fish	Medium Fish	Shark	Jelly
Phytoplankton	Zooplankton	Small Fish/Freddie	Big Fish	Shark	Turtle
Phytoplankton	Zooplankton	Baby Fish	Big Fish	Shark	Turtle
Phytoplankton	Zooplankton	Baby Fish	Big Fish	Shark	Whale
Phytoplankton	Zooplankton	Medium Fish	Big Fish	Shark	Whale

Bonus Food Chain Cards

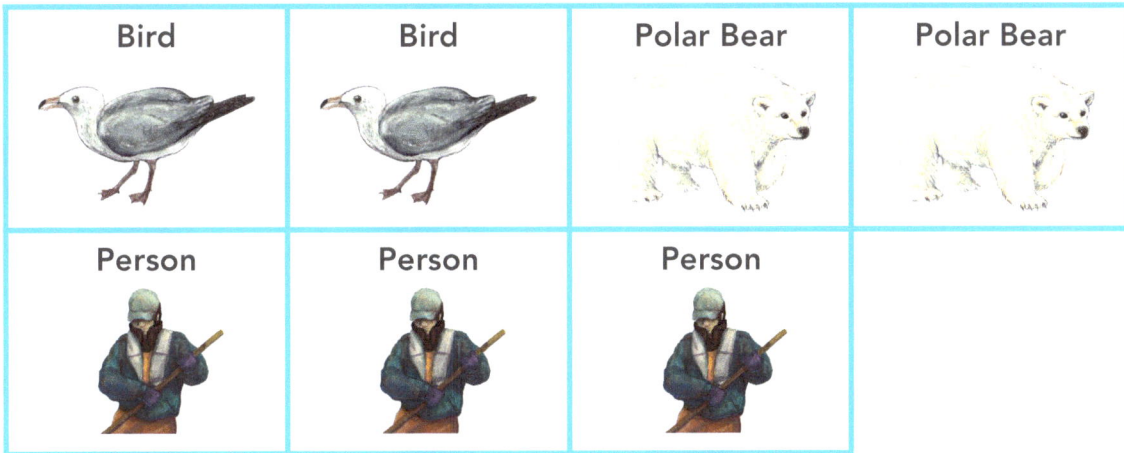

Bird	Bird	Polar Bear	Polar Bear
Person	Person	Person	

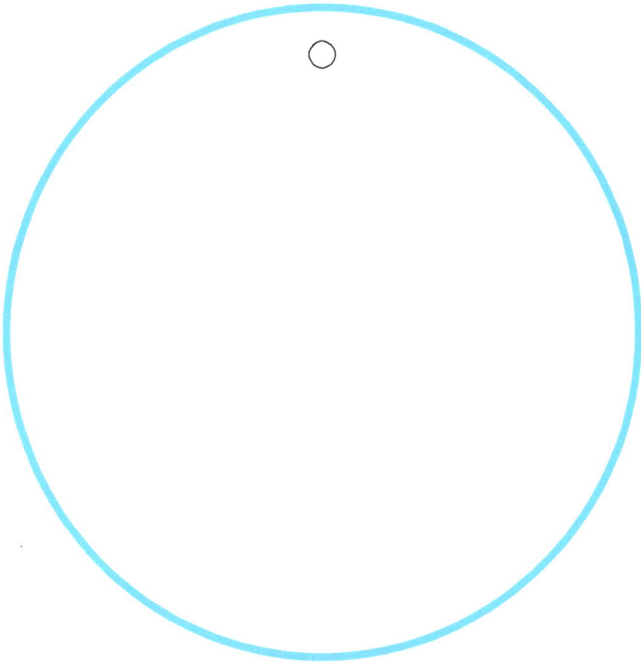

Egg or Baby

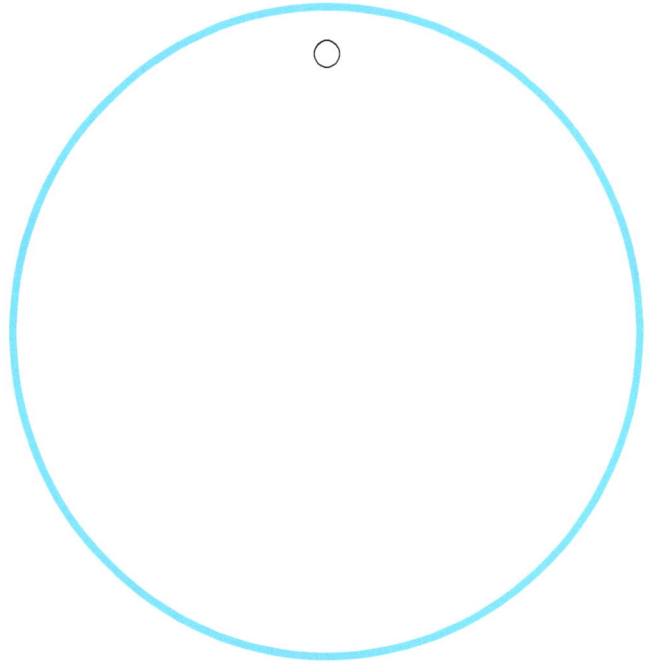

Stage 1

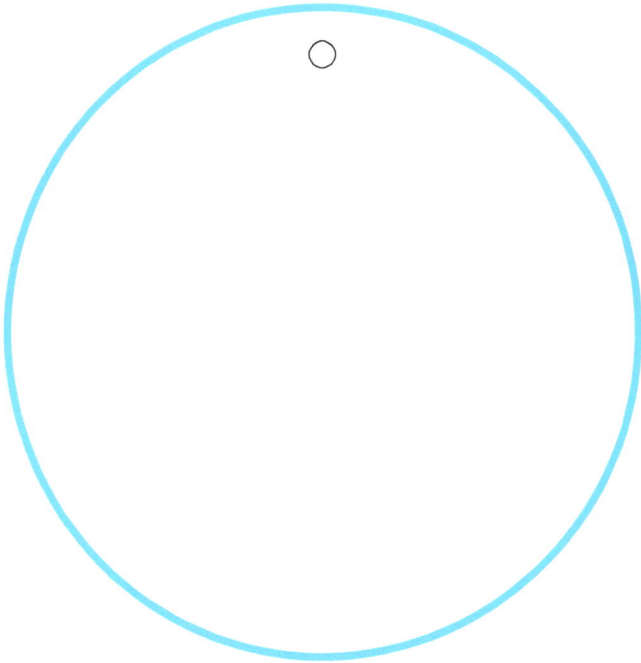

Stage 2

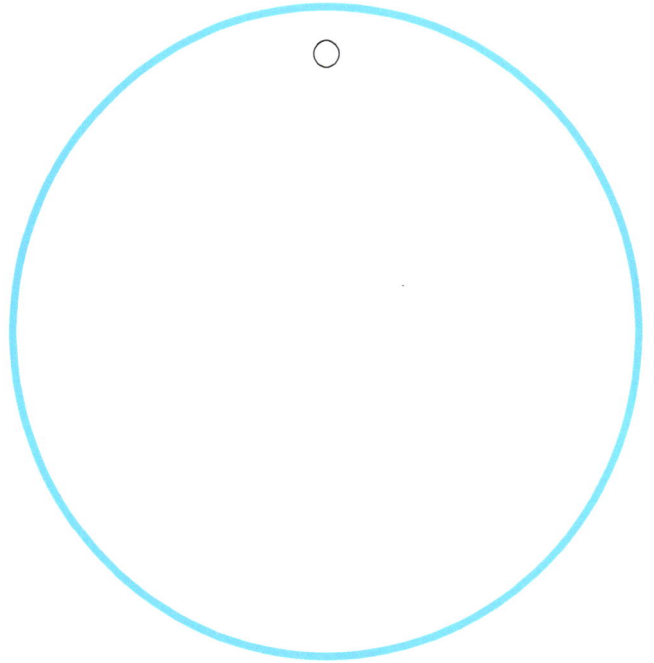

Adult

Cutouts for Activity 4: Create Your Own Metamorphosis

Science Tool Kit

www.ingramcontent.com/pod-product-compliance
Lightning Source LLC
LaVergne TN
LVHW072131070426
835513LV00002B/58

9 781942 403067